Acquiring Polish Citizenship By Descent

What You Need to Know

Neil S. Kaplan,
Founder – PolandPassport.com

Copyright © 2020 Neil S. Kaplan

All rights reserved.

FORWARD

Would you like to work, live or study in any European country? Do you want your children or grandchildren to go to a world-class university for free?

Would you like your kids to be able to work in Europe easily? Would you like to never wait in a European passport line again? How about visa free access to 127 countries including the United States?

If you have Polish (including Polish-Jewish ancestry), you may already be a Polish citizen and qualify for a Polish (European Union) passport. As you may already know, a European Union (EU) passport allows you to work, live, retire and study in any country in the European Union without limitations. So, if you can confirm your Polish citizenship a whole new world may open up for you.

The process of confirming your Polish (and EU) citizenship can be intimidating and complex.

Since 2016, our wonderful team at PolandPassport.com has worked with clients from all over the world to help them confirm their citizenship and qualify for a Polish passport. We love what we do and get great satisfaction of helping our clients in their quest for a citizenship confirmation that can change their lives.

To help you better understand this process, we have put together this book which contains questions and answers about acquiring Polish citizenship by descent.

If you have Polish ancestors but if you are not sure if you qualify

Acquiring Polish Citizenship by Descent

for Polish citizenship, you can take a short quiz about your background that we will evaluate for you free of charge: https://www.polandpassport.com/take-the-citizenship-quiz

If you do qualify, helping our Clients through this complex process is what we do. About 90% of our clients need some additional, original documents from the Polish archives beyond what they have in order to prove their case.

We are known for the outstanding quality of our legal work in Poland and our 'concierge' level of customer care worldwide.

For those questions that are not covered here, please send us an email. We will assess your situation individually and will inform you of your chances of success. These first steps are completely FREE. There is no obligation on your part to proceed with any of our services. We only charge our clients for successful outcomes and always will evaluate your personal situation without obligation or cost and with the utmost in confidentiality.

I went through this process for myself and my family and I started this business because the process can be complex and the rewards can be very high.

This book is dedicated to Adele, Natalia and the rest of our extraordinarily talented PolandPassport.com team who fight for our clients every single day.

Neil Kaplan, Founder - PolandPassport.com
Los Angeles and Warsaw
neil@polandpassport.com | February 2020.

CONTENTS

1	Advantages and Benefits of Polish Citizenship	1
2	Eligibility for Polish Citizenship by Descent	4
3	The Process of Applying for Citizenship in Poland	10
4	Obtaining Your Polish Passport After Citizenship Confirmation	14
5	Other Ways of Gaining Polish Citizenship If You Do Not Qualify for Citizenship by Descent	17
6	The PolandPassport.com Process	19
7	PolandPassport.com Costs and Pricing	23
8	Taxes	23
9	Educational Opportunities	26
10	Military Draft and Other FAQs	27
11	Creating a Legacy	29
12	Genealogy Tips	30
13	Fun Facts	32
14	About PolandPassport.com	32

1 ADVANTAGES AND BENEFITS OF POLISH CITIZENSHIP

A Polish passport gives you entry into the European Union. A Polish/European Union (EU) passport allows you to work, live, retire and study in any country in the European Union without limitations.

Other advantages include:

- Ability to **transfer your citizenship** to your children and their children.
- Unlimited **working and residential rights** in any of the 28 EU countries.
- Visa free access to 127 countries including the United States.
- Access to subsidized (often free) **college education** for yourself and your children and/or grandchildren.
- Companies that do business in Europe, have European offices or subsidiaries will see your Polish/EU passport as an advantage.

- **Qualify for jobs** that non-EU citizens cannot. In Europe, employers prefer to hire EU citizens.
- Easily **buy property** in all 27 EU member states.
- **Access to affordable healthcare** and medical care in Europe. Some EU countries have **free healthcare**.
- **Lower your tax bill** by being an EU citizen and domicile in lower tax jurisdictions.
- **Collect social benefits** reserved only for EU citizens (social security, healthcare, unemployment, pension, retirement, housing credits, et al.).
- **Start businesses with EU perks.** Get EU financing and investment incentives in 27 EU countries.

Financial Advantages

Access to banking, personal and business loans, mortgages, investment incentives reserved for EU citizens.

Everyone's priorities are different and personal, so the most important benefits vary from person to person. What is clear is that obtaining EU citizenship is a gift from you to your family for generations.

How about international banking?

Solving the nightmare for US citizens.

Easily open bank accounts globally. US citizens are often denied service at banks outside the US and are considered unattractive customers, thanks to punitive and expensive IRS reporting requirements. As a citizen of the European Union you will be welcomed as a client. You'll have access to financial institutions in countries like Switzerland, Monaco and Germany.

Want to buy property overseas?

With an EU passport, you have the right to freely purchase property in all 27 EU member states. This can be extremely cumbersome for foreigners.

2 ELIGIBILITY FOR POLISH CITIZENSHIP BY DESCENT

If your parents or grandparents are from Europe, you probably already know that EU citizenship makes it possible for you to reside, study, own property and gain employment in the European Union countries.

If you have Polish citizenship, you are already an EU citizen. Poland is a member of the EU.

If you have Polish ancestry, you can apply to have your Polish citizenship confirmed, provided you meet specific eligibility criteria. You can then apply for your Polish passport.

Specifically, the confirmation of Polish citizenship occurs after the Polish government issues a decision on your case. Persons who left Poland in the distant past or who were born abroad (as child or grandchild of Polish emigrants) have to check their Polish citizenship status to see whether or not they still hold Polish citizenship.

So, how do I know if I qualify for Polish Citizenship by Descent?

First, you need to have Polish ancestors, typically just one. They need to have been born in Poland (or an area that used to be Poland) and resided there after 1920. You will need to prove, at a minimum, that your ancestor was a Polish citizen after 1920.

Proving the citizenship of your Polish ancestor can be done in a variety of ways – typically through finding original documents related to birth, marriage, voting records or several other methods. Most of our clients have at least some of these documents such as old passports, birth and marriage records and army documents. Often times, our research team, who are intimately familiar with archives in dozens of cities and towns, will work to 'fill in the gaps.'

There are complexities in Polish citizenship law and a variety of ways that you can be disqualified including service in a foreign military, holding public office outside of Poland, adoption and a host of others.

As just a single example, you will need to provide evidence that your grandmother did not lose her citizenship by holding a public office. For instance, if she was a teacher, or public official, or any number of jobs that may be publicly funded outside of Poland, her citizenship is at risk. This is one of many exceptions and complexities in Polish citizenship law.

Generally speaking, you need to prove an unbroken 'chain' to your Polish citizen ancestor. Building this unbroken chain with original, Polish documents is the key to proving citizenship.

About 90% of our clients need some additional, original

documents from the Polish archives beyond what they have in order to prove their case.

Helping our clients through this complex process is what we do.

If you have Polish ancestors but if you are not sure if you qualify for Polish citizenship, you can take a short quiz about your background that we will evaluate for you free of charge: www.polandpassport.com/take-the-citizenship-quiz

We are known for the outstanding quality of our legal work in Poland and our 'concierge' level of customer care worldwide.

Is there a limit of generations that I can 'look back' to qualify?

No, great grandparents and beyond qualify as long as there are records confirming citizenship after 1920.

I have a Polish birth certificate from a grandparent... is that enough?

Being born in Poland or having a Polish birth certificate alone does not prove one's citizenship. Unlike the US and in many other countries, being born in Poland is not enough to prove citizenship. It is an excellent start, so hold onto that Polish birth certificate. It will certainly help.

My spouse is Polish, can I qualify?

Polish citizenship cannot be acquired through marriage, however you can reside in most EU countries with your spouse with the same rights she or he has.

How about my children or grandchildren?

If your children (or grandchildren) are under the age of 18, the applications can be submitted for all members of the family at the same time. It's important to note that each application must be completed and will be resolved based on the decision of the direct ancestor.

That means that a single mistake in any one of the applications will affect all the other applications and typically will cause all of them to be rejected.

Applying for all members of the same family at the same time makes the process faster and more efficient but requires a lot of experience and precision.

Also, every person will need to individually apply for passports. If they are 18 or older and qualify, they will need to apply separately.

There are tricky complications for children in the following circumstances:

- Adoption: Adopted children in some cases cannot claim a right to Polish citizenship through descent. Those cases have to be individually evaluated.
- Children born out of wedlock: Rules regarding citizenship for children whose parents never married are extremely complicated.

In both of these cases, there may be more options available to you that are not included here.

For more details, please contact us at info@polandpassport.com and we will evaluate your individual situation.

How about other family members? Can I use the same application?

All living family members in the direct line between you and your Polish ancestor are most likely eligible.

If you are married or have dependents, your spouse can get a residency permit to live with you. You and your children are eligible for citizenship.

Applying with siblings or cousins is a great idea. You only need one set of documents and the overall process will be more efficient.

Do I need to speak Polish to become a citizen?

You do not need to speak Polish to claim your Polish citizenship - you are only required to prove your lineage to a Polish ancestor. There is no requirement to speak Polish, however, if you decide to prepare the application on your own, you will need an advanced level of Polish language, as the whole process is carried out in Polish.

Are there any residency requirements?

No, if you are a citizen by ancestry there is no residency requirement.

Can I apply for citizenship by myself in English?

The application must be submitted in Polish. All official documentation, application forms, statements and archival records must be translated into Polish by a translator with special accreditation.

3 THE PROCESS OF APPLYING FOR CITIZENSHIP IN POLAND

To confirm Polish citizenship each person needs to provide evidence to Polish authorities that the ancestor had Polish citizenship in the first place. To do that each applying person (or designee) needs to do a search in the Polish archives in Poland. There are many different archives, some are geographically based - others, for example, that have immigration records or military service records. Proving this provenance can be a complex process.

No foreign documents are considered proof of citizenship. Only documents made in Poland by Polish authorities are sufficient. (There are exceptions for areas that are in parts of today's Ukraine or Belarus in areas that used to be part of Poland.)

About 90% of our clients need some additional, original documents from the Polish archives beyond what they have in order to prove their case.

After finding the correct documents in Poland, then all foreign documents must be translated into Polish by a translator with special accreditation.

You must have a physical representative in Poland during this process.

When that is complete then, the citizenship application must be filled out in Polish and must prove the connection between the Polish ancestor and each person applying for citizenship by descent.

Typically, you must defend the application before the Governor's Office in Warsaw and must pass the burden of proof that the citizenship wasn't lost or renounced by any of the persons applying or any family member along the hereditary chain including the ancestor. Rules about loss of citizenship are complex. Proving that someone never gave up their citizenship is frequently the longest and most time intensive part of the process - especially in larger countries (ie. US and Canada) that have a far-flung consulates.

In a complex case, that will sometimes require meetings at the Governor's office and a variety of legal motions.

A successful applicant will receive a formal citizenship declaration which is a physical document attesting to citizenship.

How long does this take?

If you have all the required documentation, the process of confirmation of citizenship can take around 9-11 months. Timing can vary significantly if more research for documents needs to be done. Because of Brexit, the queue is particularly long right now. There is often significant variability on timing of cases. Beware of anyone who assure you that this can be done in a shorter timeframe.

Will I need to go to Poland?

No. If you are a Polish citizen by ancestry, there is no residency requirement nor are you required to go to Poland at any time during or after this process.

Is it possible to do all the work myself and not hire counsel to help?

You can do this yourself via your local consulate. It can be very challenging. So much so that it is the main reason we have a thriving business advocating for our clients through what is most often a cumbersome process.

As an example: You will have to navigate your way, in Polish, through Polish laws, regulations and bureaucracy. You must nominate a resident of Poland to act on your behalf; There are many opportunities for error and delay in the process.

4 OBTAINING YOUR POLISH PASSPORT AFTER CITIZENSHIP CONFIRMATION

As discussed previously, a successful applicant will receive a formal citizenship declaration which is a physical document attesting to citizenship.

After a decision confirming citizenship is issued, the new citizen must apply for a Polish version of vital records to be issued by Polish Civil Records Office (in other words, a Polish birth certificate and marriage certificate). That stage is often overlooked and is critical. Mistakes in application or inconsistencies in these documents may lead to inability to obtain your passport.

This is a prerequisite to obtaining a Polish passport and there is no possibility to apply for the document without Polish vital records. We have seen many frustrated people who actually have been declared citizens but cannot obtain passports through complexities in this area. This is an area where we have deep knowledge.

To apply for a Polish passport you need to be a citizen of Poland. You also need to have your birth certificate registered in Poland and you need to have a PESEL number (a Polish identification number similar to a US Social Security number). After your citizenship is confirmed, you then fill out your passport application (in Polish of course) which you will need to submit to a Polish consulate or embassy.

Helping our clients through this process in a structured, detailed process is the core of what we do.

Usually two visits to a Polish Consulate/Embassy are required to obtain a passport. <u>An application for a new passport</u> **<u>must be submitted in person.</u>** During the first visit the application is filed and fingerprints are taken. The second visit includes picking up the passport. Some consulates allow delivery by registered mail in lieu of the second appointment, if that is an option at your consulate, additional payment will be required. You will have to ask if this mailing option is available.

What types of passports are there?

Poland issues passports valid for 10 years for adults, 5 years for children. They are produced in Poland and contain biometric features including fingerprints and a chip. This type of passport typically gets you expedited exit and entry at EU airports. It's a huge time saver.

In an emergency, you can apply for an interim passport, valid for 12 months and produced by the Polish consulate locally. In urgent cases, the interim passport can be issued within 24 hours.

How do I apply for a passport for my child?

The child must also go through the process of being declared a citizen first. This does not happen 'automatically'.

Both parents must be present to submit the passport application, unless there is a court decision restricting the parental authority of one of the parents. For complicated cases, please ask us.

How long does it take to get a passport after gaining citizenship?

Typical processing time is around 2 months but varies at different consulates around the world. Emergency passports can be generated more quickly.

5 OTHER WAYS OF GAINING POLISH CITIZENSHIP IF YOU DO NOT QUALIFY FOR CITIZENSHIP BY DESCENT

If you are not eligible for citizenship through the normal channels, there is a process whereby you can appeal directly to the President of Poland for an exemption. The President of Poland may grant Polish citizenship to any foreigner. The process is called "Granting."

The Granting procedure has several requirements.

The application must be completed in Polish and all the documents you will submit with it (such as your birth certificate) needs to be translated or transcribed to Polish by a translator with special accreditation. Chances for obtaining citizenship by granting are difficult to predict. The President of Poland is not obligated to grant citizenship to anyone. A well prepared case, professionally done, has the highest chance of success.

PolandPassport.com does handle some of these applications

on a case-by-case basis. Please contact us if you are interested in learning more about this process.

6 THE POLANDPASSPORT.COM PROCESS

Our business helps our clients gain Polish citizenship and helps them with the process of obtaining their passports.

How does your process work?

Here is what happens if you proceed:

As everyone's circumstances are different, we have to assess your situation individually. Once we have gained a better understanding of your situation, we will inform you of your chances of success. Again, this is completely free and there is no obligation on your part to proceed with any of our services.

You will need to give us some basic information about yourself and your family with our short qualification quiz. We will send you an email, often asking for more detailed family tree information, and then we will give you our assessment of your eligibility.

These first steps are completely FREE. There is no obligation on your part to proceed with any of our services.

Your first steps toward an EU passport:

Step 1: Fill out the qualification quiz on PolandPassport.com asking basic information about yourself and your family.

Step 2: We will evaluate your survey to assess eligibility and the likelihood of your success. After this evaluation (usually completed within a few days), we will send you an email informing you if you might qualify for Polish citizenship. A detailed explanation of our services as well as the path to EU citizenship will be outlined in the confirmation email. We may email you to ask some more questions. There is no obligation to proceed.

Step 3: If you like what we have to say, hire us and we will do everything we can to untangle the complicated process for you and make becoming a Polish citizen as smooth as possible.

About 90% of our clients need some additional, original documents from the Polish archives beyond what they have in order to prove their case.

Do you only work with USA clients?

No. We have clients from many countries.

Can I do this myself?

Here are some of the issues that you may face in tackling this on your own. About 20% of our clients are 'do-it-yourself' returnees.

First, you will need the help of a Polish consulate or embassy and someone in Poland. There will be a variety of fees involved throughout the process (all of which are covered in our fee).

Local consulates and embassies often send your applications back to Poland where they are reviewed via diplomatic mail and the frequency of how long that takes is variable, so you will not know how long your application might sit without progress.

You will likely need to have a representative in Poland to receive correspondence in the event that the Governor's Office issues a request for documents or clarifications in your case – this happens frequently and can also cause long delays.

With all due respect to the hard working government officials in consulates around the world, the knowledge and experience in these offices can be variable regarding citizenship law and we do talk to people who have been given conflicting or inaccurate information.

Confirmation of citizenship is not enough to obtain a passport. You also have to go through a procedure to transcribe your birth certificate in the Polish Civil Records office. (This entire process including the issuance of the certificate is also included in our fees).

Timing becomes an issue again here as it can take a long time to get the document to Poland via the consulate, and if there any doubts or questions (which happens frequently) you would have to wait for the civil records office to contact your representative or have the communication routed again through the consulate. Again, everything in Polish, of course.

Our process is typically much faster as we have a team in Warsaw that visits the Governor's office weekly (our office is also in Warsaw). Our Los Angeles office is convenient to a consulate as well and we are there often.

We have a legal team with experience to plan your application, researchers to track down archival documents needed to support your application, attorneys to defend your application in Poland, and document specialists to help track down the documents you will need to complete the "chain" of ancestry between you and your Polish ancestor. Many of these functions simply cannot be performed by a consulate or embassy.

7 POLANDPASSPORT.COM COSTS AND PRICING

How much? Well, it depends. Some cases are hard and some not as hard. During our assessment we will determine and quote a specific fixed price that we charge only for successful outcomes.

We also offer discounts for siblings, children and other family members as it is efficient for us to do more than one case concurrently from the same family.

As everyone's circumstances are unique, we will assess your situation individually and will inform you of your chances of success. These first steps are completely FREE. There is no obligation on your part to proceed with any of our services.

8 TAXES

We are not tax attorneys and do not give tax advice. For your specific circumstances please engage your own counsel.

Most countries have signed bilateral agreements whereby you only pay tax in one country. For a US citizen there are generally no tax issues related to this unless you begin working in the EU.

Polish citizens who are non-residents (live outside of Poland) and who do not work in Poland, are not typically required to pay Polish taxes.

Here is a summary of the official statement that is used to describe the situation In Poland. If Poland is not your home (ie. your family is not here, you just have the passport) and at the same time you are not here for more than 183 days during the course of a calendar year, there's no tax residence and because of that no tax obligations. If you do earn money in Poland then you would have to pay tax, but *just from the income that was created in Poland.*

Here is the citation from Polish law.

dana osoba fizyczna nie posiada w Polsce centrum interesów osobistych lub gospodarczych (ośrodka interesów życiowych) i-przebywa na terytorium Polski nie więcej niż 183 dni w roku podatkowym (rozumianym jako rok kalendarzowy),wówczas nie jest rezydentem i zapłaci w Polsce podatek wyłącznie od dochodów uzyskanych na terytorium Polski.Nie będzie natomiast zobowiązana do zapłacenia w Polsce podatku od dochodów zagranicznych.natomiast osoba nie posiadająca w Polsce swego ośrodka interesów osobistych ani gospodarczych i nie przebywająca w kraju więcej niż 183 dni w roku podatkowym, nie jest uznawana za polskiego rezydenta podatkowego i na terytorium Polski nie ciąży na niej żaden obowiązek podatkowy z tytułu dochodów uzyskanych w innych krajach.

9 EDUCATIONAL OPPORTUNITIES

Free or low cost education for your children and grandchildren.

For anyone with young children, planning to have children, or with grandchildren - you can give future generations the gift of free, affordable university education in Europe...by simply confirming your Polish citizenship which will allow you to get an EU passport.

- Free university education in many European countries.
- Subsidized tuition rates at world class universities.
- Access to scholarships reserved for EU citizens.
- Cheaper alternatives for medical and law schools at world class universities.
- With Polish citizenship, you and your children will be able to study in Europe and pay European Union tuition rates at European universities.
- Many universities in Europe are completely free for

citizens of the European Union.

10 MILITARY DRAFT AND OTHER FAQS

Does it matter where I live?

No.

Can I hold dual citizenship?

Yes. Most countries, including UK, US, Canada, Australia, Israel, New Zealand and South Africa allow you to have dual or multiple citizenships.

Do I have to renounce my current citizenship?

In most countries, including the US, having another country's citizenship does not affect your current citizenship. Please check regulations with your local authorities.

Can I live and work in other EU countries?

Yes. Having a Polish passport is like having a passport to any EU country, allowing you to live and work anywhere in the EU.

What countries are in the EU?

Member countries include Austria, Belgium, Bulgaria, Croatia, Cyprus, Czech Republic, Denmark, Estonia, Finland, France, Germany, Greece, Hungary, Ireland, Italy, Latvia, Lithuania, Luxembourg, Malta, Netherlands, Poland, Portugal, Romania, Slovakia, Slovenia, Spain, Sweden. Passports issued in those countries are EU passports.

What about Brexit?

As of April 2020, (this book's publication date) Polish citizens' ability to move to or work in the UK has not changed.

What about security clearance in my home country?

We are not qualified to answer this question.

What is an apostille?

The Apostille is usually a stamp (or a sticker) placed on original documents to confirm their authenticity. Countries that are signatories to the Hague Convention of 5 October 1961 are required to present their official documents accompanied by Apostilles. Birth, death and marriage certificates, notarial deeds, court documents, sworn translations and other official documents need to be Apostilled before they can be submitted to other Hague Convention signatory countries. We often will need this stamp to officially process your documents.

Is there a requirement for military service or draft registration?

No.

11 CREATING A LEGACY

The Gift that Keeps on Giving!

By becoming a Polish citizen, you will pass on Polish citizenship to your children at birth. And they will automatically pass on their Polish citizenship to their children at birth. It really is a gift that goes on for generations and the benefits of European Citizenship will continue long into the future.

It's about work or creating unique experiences for their kids.

Polish dual citizenship allows you to live and work unrestricted and for unlimited time in the European Union. You'll never have to worry about a work visa or getting "sponsored" by a European company before working in the EU - as an EU citizen, you can do so automatically. You can live anywhere in the European Union for as long as you want, completely unrestricted. If you are married or have dependents, your family gains many of these rights as well.

12 GENEALOGY TIPS

Write down your own name, birth date, place of birth, parents, and spouse, if married, date of marriage, place of marriage, children's complete names and their dates of birth. After you do your own family, do your parents, grandparents and so on.

The family tree will give you a clear perspective of what you know, who is related to whom and what you are missing for each individual. There are many software packages available to help you create a family tree, or you can look online for free "family tree" or "pedigree chart" templates.

You can also do it in a simple spreadsheet or even draw it up by hand. Start with the basic details: name at birth, date and location of birth, date and location of marriage, and names of children. If you find out more, and it interests you, add notes regarding education, profession, and any interesting stories. Those last details not only are interesting, they also may be valuable to know regarding your Polish ancestors.

It's worth assessing old photos, letters and records as they can contain many helpful details. Look for dates, names and any other useful information. Don't forget envelopes and inscriptions on backs of photos. Anything in your possession can contain clues: birth certificates, marriage certificates, death certificates, naturalization certificates, army registrations, travel documents, et al.

13 FUN FACTS

In the most recent elections held in the EU, more than 2,000 EU citizens stood as candidates in the member state where they resided without having the nationality of that state.

Over 14 million EU citizens reside in another member state. Free movement – or the ability to live, work or study anywhere in the Union – is the EU right most cherished by Europeans.

Erasmus+ will enable over 4 million European students over the next 5 years to have education or training experiences abroad. Check it out!

EU citizens rely on being protected by a comprehensive set of passenger rights when travelling by air, rail, ship or bus. In certain circumstances, you get compensation in cases of cancellation or delay.

EU citizens get extra protection if you buy package holidays including rights to cancellation without penalties and protection if a tour operator or airline goes bankrupt.

EU citizens can go to any other EU member state's consulate or embassy to ask for help when you travel to a country outside the EU and your home country is not represented. EU member states must help citizens of other member states to leave a country in crisis situations.

You can contact the European Direct Contact Centre which answers all sorts of questions on EU-related matters by email or phone. You can also visit the Direct Information Centres which are throughout Europe.

EU citizens can vote and be a candidate in European Parliament elections in the EU country that you reside, under the same conditions as the nationals of that country.

EU citizens can vote and be a candidate in national elections in the EU country where you reside under the same conditions as the nationals of that country.

In 14 member states, an EU citizen may become the mayor of the municipality where he or she resides, without being a national of that country.

You can use the website Your Europe for practical information and your rights when moving, living, studying, training, working, shopping or travelling abroad.

You can dial 112, the EU emergency number, free from any mobile or landline phone everywhere in the EU. Operators speak a variety of languages and will put you through to the right emergency service.

14 ABOUT POLANDPASSPORT.COM

Neil Kaplan, founder of PolandPassport.com, is a long time Los Angeles based senior executive with a reputation for honesty and hard work. His career includes time at Bain and Company, CBS, the Los Angeles Times and Universal Studios Hollywood.

Having successfully navigated Polish citizenship for his mother, himself and three of his children, Neil understands both the challenges of navigating this cumbersome process and the rewards of success. He is dedicated to helping others down this same path of helping people of Polish descent from various countries in receiving Polish citizenship and a Polish EU passport.

We have a Warsaw based legal team with experience to plan your application, researchers throughout the country to track down archival documents needed to support your application, attorneys to defend your application in Poland, and document specialists to help track down the documents you will need to complete the "chain" of ancestry between you and your Polish ancestor.

How much do you charge?

It depends on the complexity of your case. Quotes are free without obligation. All cases are priced individually.

If you have detailed knowledge of your family's history and have access to documentation proving your ancestry such as Polish passports, birth certificates, army records and other historical materials, we can easily provide an all-inclusive free no obligation quote for our services.

We only charge for successful outcomes.

Why should I trust you with my information?

We have strict policies and procedures in place to assure your personal information and documents are treated in confidence. We never share any information with anyone unless expressly authorized by you.

Where are you located and what is your phone number and email address?

Our US Headquarters is in Torrance, California (near Los Angeles). We have a team of researchers and attorneys in Warsaw, Poland. Our phone number is +1 424 307 4079. Contact us at info@polandpassport.com. We are known for our 'concierge' level of customer care.

Made in the USA
Coppell, TX
25 June 2022

79239014R00025